This book is dedicated
with love and appreciation
for our dearly departed poet friends.
They have helped to bring
the promise of hope
into the lives of so many and
will continue to spread
His love through their verses.

**The intent and
purpose of this volume is to
give you faith, hope and
inspiration. Hopefully it will help bring
peace and tranquility into your life. May
it be a reminder of God's love, guidance
and His many blessings.**

**Our publications help to support our work
for needy children in over 120 countries
around the world. Through our
programs, thousands of children are
fed, clothed, educated, sheltered
and given the opportunity to
live decent lives.**

Salesian Missions wishes to extend special thanks and gratitude to o
generous poet friends and to the publishers who have given us permission to repri
material included in this book. Every effort has been made to give prop
acknowledgments. Any omissions or errors are deeply regretted, and the publisher, up
notification, will be pleased to make the necessary corrections in subsequent editions

Cover photo Monarch Butterfly on Pink Asters, Dietrick Photography

First Edition Printed in the U.S.A. by Concord Litho Group, Concord, NH 03301.

The Promise of Hope
from the Salesian Collection

Compiled and edited by
Jennifer Grimaldi

Illustrated by
Russell Bushée, Frank Massa,
Paul Scully, Robert Van Steinburg,
Maureen McCarthy, Gail L. Pepin
and Helen M. L. Kunic

Contents

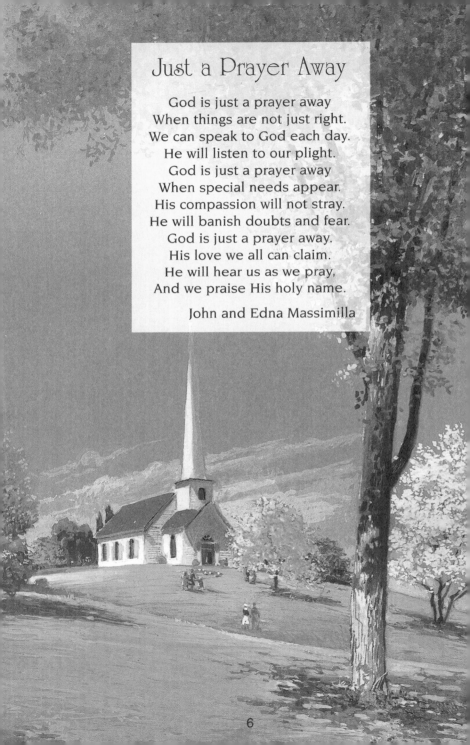

Just a Prayer Away

God is just a prayer away
When things are not just right.
We can speak to God each day.
He will listen to our plight.
God is just a prayer away
When special needs appear.
His compassion will not stray.
He will banish doubts and fear.
God is just a prayer away.
His love we all can claim.
He will hear us as we pray,
And we praise His holy name.

John and Edna Massimilla

The Word
Not Spoken

Be kind to each other,
For life is so short;
Be loving and thoughtful.
Have a good heart.

Never end the day
When you're of a bad mind;
Be close to each other.
Be thankful and kind.

Remember the good things,
The fine younger years;
Recall of the past
The grace of your peers.

You will never be sorry
You said the good word;
There is nothing sadder than
A word not spoken… the word not heard.

James Joseph Huesgen

Encourage your hearts and
strengthen them in every
good deed and word.
2 Thessalonians 2:17

For Lovely Things

I thank You, God, for lovely things:
For sunshine bright, each bird that sings,
For beauty that the springtime brings…

For fragrant roses kissed by dew,
For smiling skies of azure blue,
For loyal friends both old and new…

For Autumn foliage aglow,
For moonlight on new-fallen snow,
For awesome sunset's crimson glow…

For every mother's love so dear,
For letters bringing me such cheer,
For sweet content as night draws near…

For golden deeds that say, "I care,"
For rainbows with their colors fair,
For quiet time I spend in prayer…

For tulips bursting through the sod,
For peace along the path I trod,
For lovely things… I thank You, God.

Beverly J. Anderson

How lovely Your dwelling,
O Lord of hosts!
Psalm 84:2

9

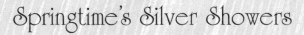

Springtime's Silver Showers

The wild, sweet rain of springtime spills
On pale blue larkspur on the hills,
On apple-tree blossoms and leaf-green bough,
On wildflowers' sheen from rain-silvered showers.
Rain scrubs the sunflower's golden face
And shines the meadow grass in place,
Golden daffodils sprinkled through the haze
Unveil these precious springtime days.
Mist sweeps the woods where lilies grow
And leaves God's radiant world aglow.
This bright, green earth, blue skies above,
Present the wonder of God's glorious love.

Elisabeth Weaver Winstead

The Rain
Came to Call

This morning was cloudy,
The rain came to call,
Refreshing the flowers,
Gave beauty to all.

It seems that the rain has
Put them all on display.
They hold their heads higher,
Look lovely this way.

The rain sure was welcome,
It had been a long time.
The earth needed moisture;
The sun soon will shine.

And today I'm so thankful
For the much-needed rain.
There is beauty and splendor…
It's the earth's latest gain.

Katherine Smith Matheney

Who covers the heavens with clouds,
provides rain for the earth, makes
grass sprout on the mountains.
Psalm 147:8

The Gift

A garden is a gift from God
To cheer and lift the heart;
A tiny glimpse of paradise
Of which we'll have a part.

Our eyes can feast on beauty
Of rainbow-colored flowers,
Where birds are sweetly singing,
We spend many happy hours.

As we look up to Heaven
To skies so blue and clear,
Our ears can feast on lovely sounds
That fall upon the ear.

No artist can paint pictures
Of the beauty that we see,
'Tis painted by God's finger;
This gift to all is free.

When I walk in my garden
'Mid its symphony of praise,
I never want to leave it
For all my earthly days.

I meet God in my garden,
From cares I am released,
And there we walk together
And my heart is filled with peace.

Helen Gleason

Beautiful Summertime

Summer takes a beauty bath
On a rosy, sunburned path.
She dons her cotton-colored hat
And stops by a daisy for a chat.

Summer babbles by a brook
And lingers in a shady nook,
Till a noisy nightingale
Did her serenade regale.

Summer in delightful bliss
Charms me with her sunny kiss,
Then she wanders on her way
So autumntime can have her day.

Nora M. Bozeman

Toilworn and Weary

Toilworn and weary I come, Lord,
Resting my head on Thy breast –
Too wounded and tired for words
And my teardrops nearing their crest.
Toilworn and weary I come, Lord,
Just like You've asked me to –
I've nothing left for resources
…I'm giving it all up to You.
Toilworn and weary I come, Lord,
Oh, haste to comfort Thy child!
I need the arms of my Father
To hold me so tender and mild.
Toilworn and weary I come, Lord,
And faithful You've proven to be!
Once more my bruised heart has been mended
…And drawn so much closer to Thee!

Denise A. DeWald

*They that hope in the Lord will renew
their strength, they will soar as with
eagles' wings; They will run and not
grow weary, walk and not grow faint.*
Isaiah 40:31

God's Generosity

God is giving blessings.
Reach up and just receive.
His hand is open to our need
If we but believe.
His generosity is great.
God loves to give and give.
Giving is God's way of life.
It's just the way to live.
Our hearts are full of thanks to Him.
We sing Him all our praise.
We commit our lives to God
All of our blessed days.

Carol Zileski

Boys and Dogs

A boy, a dog and a Summer day
Are Nature's recipe
For making an adventure
And a golden memory.

The world's a stage for boys and dogs,
For every day is new
Filled with endless possibilities
For both of them to do.

Theirs is a world of make-believe,
For secrets shared by two,
On country roads or seaside walks
Where fondest dreams come true.

A boy, a dog and a Summer day
Are childhood's smiling face
In the mirror of antiquity
That time cannot erase.

Clay Harrison

*With my whole being I sing endless
praise to You. O Lord, my God,
forever will I give You thanks.*
Psalm 30:13

17

He Leadeth Me

He gently leads me along life's journey
And guides every single step that I take.
Whether beside still waters or raging seas,
I know that His child He'll never forsake.

He is my Shepherd and I am His sheep;
I shall follow wherever His footsteps roam.
Great peace and joy He brings to me,
And one day His hand shall lead me home.

I shall fear no evil when He comes for me,
For He loves me with heart and soul.
His rod and staff shall point the way,
And I shall tread where gleams the gold.

Goodness and mercy shall follow me home,
My cup will overflow with joy, full and free.
I shall dwell in the Lord's house evermore;
Oh, blessed thought... He leadeth me!

Barbara Cagle Ray

Sands of Life

The seconds tick, the minutes fly,
The hours roll… a day has passed.
The night has bid the day goodbye;
The sands of life are flowing fast!

A week is gone – a month, a year –
Still life is passed and gone.
On life's horizon does appear
A new and brilliant dawn.

The sands of life are flowing fast,
But when the Lord is near,
His holy light bedims the past
And all shadows disappear!

Clayton G. Moseley

*The sand of the seashore, the
drops of rain, the days of eternity:
who can number these?*
Sirach 1:2

Sharing God's Gifts

It's really quite amazing
What a kind word can do
To someone who is troubled,
Downhearted, sad and blue.

We can lift their sunken spirits
In a way God has designed
By following His teachings
And being merciful and kind.

Life isn't very pleasant
When tears are bittersweet,
Yet we can help those in distress
To conquer and defeat.

Give them plenty of encouragement,
A handshake and a smile,
Then lift them up to God in prayer
To help them through their trial.

Kindness is a gift from God
That He means for us to share
With those who are less fortunate
To show them that we care.

Shirley Hile Powell

*Bless the Lord, my soul; do not
forget all the gifts of God.*
Psalm 103:2

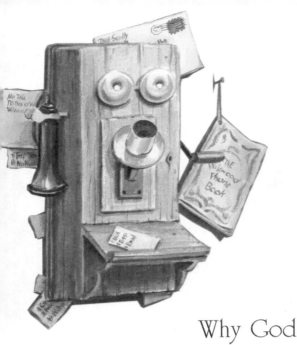

Why God Created Friendship

God created friendship,
For it comes directly from the heart,
Like a pulse you oft can feel it beating
Right from the very start!
A deed done out of kindness,
A word of wisdom spoken to steer,
A cup of tea offered from generosity,
And a hug of tenderness to wipe away a tear.
Somebody to take the time to visit
And chat for hours when the weather's bad,
Sharing each moment and memory –
Both the happy and sad.
Why did God create friendship?
Perhaps to supply a listening ear
To comfort a heart that's aching
And to provide a few chuckles and cheers!

Linda C. Grazulis

His Gifts

The day is passed, the night is still.
Soft stars twinkle over distant hills.
The day's events I soon recall
And see that You are Lord of all.
You gave me shelter from the storm,
Food and clothes to keep me warm,
A family's ever-loving care,
Hope in place of my despair.
Friends to help me on the way,
Time enough to sit and pray,
Earth and all its beauty fair...
Thank You, God, I know You care.

Mary Ann Jameson

*I would soon find a
shelter from the raging
wind and storm.*
Psalm 55:9

Because You Are My Friend

I'm glad we met, dear friend,
On that day so long ago.
"By chance," we said, and yet I think
That God has willed it so.

Your friendly way has brought me cheer,
The thoughtful things you do;
It means so much to have a friend
Who's always warm and true.

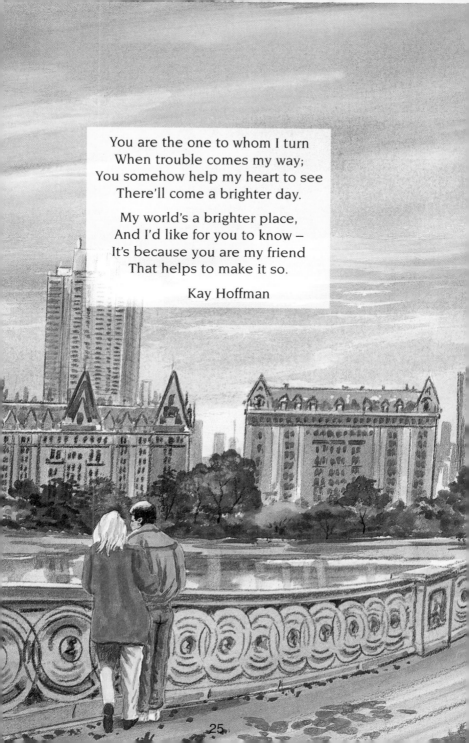

You are the one to whom I turn
When trouble comes my way;
You somehow help my heart to see
There'll come a brighter day.

My world's a brighter place,
And I'd like for you to know –
It's because you are my friend
That helps to make it so.

Kay Hoffman

25

I'm Tying the Leaves

Oh, I'm tying the leaves
So they won't come down,
So Summer won't go away,
For the best time of year
Is when voices we hear
Of children so hard at play.
Through the meadows they run,
Unaware 'neath the sun
That Summer's about to fade,
So I'm tying the leaves
That they won't come down
So Summer won't go away.
Oh, I'm tying the leaves
So they won't fall down,
So Summer won't go away;
Now the wildflowers bloom
And the birds sing in tune
'Neath summery sunshine rays.
But the Summer must go
So that cold winds might blow;
God fashioned it so that way.
Still I dream tying leaves
That they won't come down
So Summer won't go away.

Loise Pinkerton Fritz

And He changeth the times
and the seasons…
Daniel 2:21

Metamorphosis

Today I noticed a leaf turning gold –
It's Nature's signal of approaching Fall.
Rose's petals float skyward on the wind,
As Summer bids a sweet adieu to all.

The goldenrod has lost its vivid color;
There's a crispness in the northern breeze.
Daylight hours are becoming shorter now;
Crimson bonnets will soon adorn the trees.

Golden sunlight crowns the changing leaves,
As Summer says farewell to flickering green.
School bells will toll for the children soon;
I can almost hear their familiar ring!

The grand Designer stands in the shadows
With His paintbrush ready for the task.
Summer sings her sweet farewell refrain;
The earth is soon with brilliance massed!

Barbara Cagle Ray

To Someone Very Near

Though many miles lie in between
The two of us today,
Somehow I feel that you can hear
The things I cannot say.
And though it is not given me
To walk the path you trod,
Each day we meet in prayer before
The golden throne of God.

Nobody knows how long or short
Our time on earth will be.
That's why today I want to say
How much you mean to me.
I know you're always there for me
Just as I'm here for you,
For everybody needs someone
To tell their troubles to.

Life's little disappointments
Have somehow lost their sting,
And I'm a better person
For the friendship that you bring,
And though some dreams did not come true
And some loved ones have gone,
Together we can lift the cross
We could not bear alone.

Grace E. Easley

Autumn's Golden Days

The golden days of Autumn blaze
Across the land in russet haze.
A treasure chest of gold and red
Along the ground the wind has spread.

The Autumn sun setting low
Regales the sky in crimson glow.
Frost falls on orange-pumpkin days
And lights bright harvest-moon displays.

Autumn's like a beauty queen
Gowned in red and gold and green.
She gathers accolades and then
Disappears till it's Fall again.

Nora M. Bozeman

*As long as the earth lasts,
seedtime and harvest, cold and
heat, Summer and Winter, and
day and night shall not cease.*
Genesis 8:22

Golden Autumn

Golden Autumn!
How it wraps its glory 'round us,
The glory of the harvest of the year,
When the springtime planting comes to full fruitation,
When the days and nights are cool and crispy clear.

Golden Autumn!
How the Midas touch prevails now
At this season of the falling of the year,
When the large and mellow moon creeps o'er the mountain
And attuned to sounds of harvest is each ear.

Golden Autumn!
How its presence sets us singing,
Singing praises to the God who reigns above,
Giving thanks for every beauty and provision
He affords us through His mercy and His love.

Loise Pinkerton Fritz

From Walls to Bridges

If you can open up your heart
And let your love shine through…
God will fill you with His grace
And He'll draw close to you.

If you can share your very soul
With others on your way…
Loneliness will disappear
And peace will come to stay.

God planned for us to build a bridge
To reach the other side…
Forming friendships as we go
And choosing not to hide.

Building walls can lock us in
And keep God's blessings out...
A heart that's closed can never learn
What love is all about.

Don't be afraid of what you'll find,
Just let those walls come down...
Cross the bridge to the other side;
Love waits on holy ground.

Jill Lemming

*Therefore my heart is glad,
my soul rejoices; my body
also dwells secure.*
Psalm 16:9

Kindness

Kindness is a Christian virtue
That is blessed upon our hearts
To be shown to one another
As Lord Jesus would impart.
For in giving of our persons
Or in giving of our stores,
We do service to our Savior
In a fashion He adores;
And it does not really matter
How we proffer to be kind,
But that every act of kindness
Leaves a touch of love behind.

Michael Dubina

Victory Over All

When roads ahead are rocky,
God is holding out His hand;
When no one else is listening,
He's there to understand.
When life is giving sorrow –
Foreboding, full of pain –
God offers His protection
And wipes away the stain.
His love is always waiting
To fill our days with joy;
His strength is quite sufficient
To conquer any ploy.
And God is always ready
To lift us when we fall;
By trusting Him, we all can be
The victors over all.

Bonnie L. Nelson

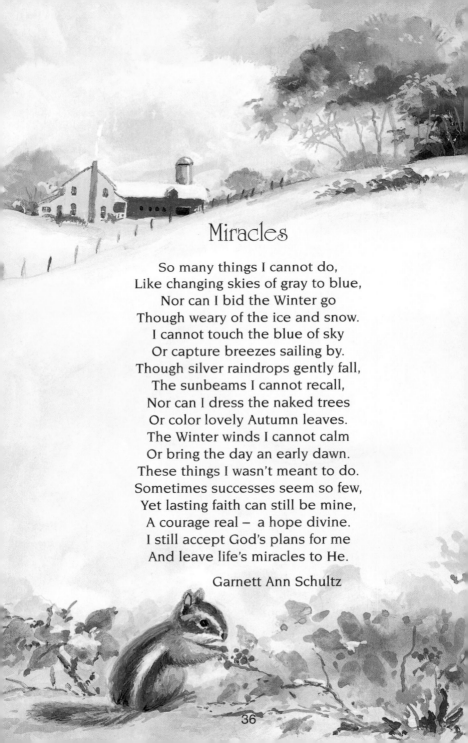

Miracles

So many things I cannot do,
Like changing skies of gray to blue,
Nor can I bid the Winter go
Though weary of the ice and snow.
I cannot touch the blue of sky
Or capture breezes sailing by.
Though silver raindrops gently fall,
The sunbeams I cannot recall,
Nor can I dress the naked trees
Or color lovely Autumn leaves.
The Winter winds I cannot calm
Or bring the day an early dawn.
These things I wasn't meant to do.
Sometimes successes seem so few,
Yet lasting faith can still be mine,
A courage real – a hope divine.
I still accept God's plans for me
And leave life's miracles to He.

Garnett Ann Schultz

Night Snows

In peaceful stillness of night,
The wonder begins to unfold,
Fluttering in gentle flight,
Settling in drifts of white gold.

Glimmering in the morning light,
Reflecting the sun's bright rays,
Crystallizing into patches of ice
Before slowly melting away.

The Lord has made this glorious show
For His children everywhere.
A morning full of liquid snow
With drifting flakes in midair.

Rebecca Sweeney

*My people will live in peaceful
country, in secure dwellings
and quiet resting places.*
Isaiah 32:18

Friends Forever

Friends forever, that's how it is
When lonely hearts connect
And share the ups and downs of life
With honor and respect.

Friends are there in time of need
To comfort and console.
Their bond becomes the anodyne
That makes the wounded whole.

Friends see beyond the obvious,
Forgiving our mistakes,
Because they know and understand
How quickly hearts can break.

Friends share our joys and sorrows
When no one seems to care,
And with a friend beside us,
The weather's always fair.

Friends forever, how sweet the voice
That unlocks our door.
The voice that simply says, "I care!"
And that's what friends are for!

Clay Harrison

Faith

Faith misses the storm,
Sees only the sun,
Forgets about clouds
Or things left undone.
Just courage and trust,
No doubts and no fears,
And no questions why
And no bitter tears.
Faith is believing
In things still unknown,
Accepting each challenge
Though oft all alone.
It's trusting tomorrow
Despite hurts or trials,
It's patience – endeavors –
And sharing life's smiles.
It's looking ahead
Into things yet to be,
A soul filled with goodness
A mind bright and free.
It's living each day,
Every heartache or sorrow…
Faith is the reason
We welcome tomorrow.

Garnett Ann Schultz

Winter Snowflowers

Twinkling snowflakes swirl into my hands –
Small, glistening, sparkling gems,
Fragile, crystal, frosted flowerlets,
With jeweled petals, but no stems.

Mistletoe, cedar, spruce, holly and fir
Show beautiful greenery in Nature's design.
Goldfinches, song sparrows and merry chickadees
Send forth a concert from each snow-laden pine.

I gaze at the shimmering, vibrant sheen,
Snowflowers afloat like castles in dreams,
Sparkling white blossoms in star-flake design…
God brightens the night with His spun-silver beams.

Elisabeth Weaver Winstead

You are my lamp, O Lord,
O my God, You brighten
the darkness about me.
2 Samuel 22:29

41

Winter Winds

Winter winds catch earth unguarded
With a fury wild and free
And undress most of Nature,
Making changes quite rapidly.

My breath seems almost frozen
During the cold Winter days,
Yet I love the frozen silence
And watching the children play.

Pine boughs are snow-covered
And a resting place for squirrels,
While around this picturesque setting,
Winds blow snow around in swirls.

The fields look brown and desolate
And the barren trees so forlorn;
Then snowflakes are ushered in
And both are beautifully adorned.

Winds whistle their Winter melodies
Through the cold and deserted trees,
While the fire crackles in the fireplace,
Shutting out the frigid Winter freeze.

Shirley Hile Powell

*When you lie down, you need not
be afraid, when you rest, your
sleep will be sweet.*
Proverbs 3:24

Doubt

Just above the darkest clouds,
The sun is shining clear.
A sign that God, who made the sun,
Is always, ever near.

Don't give up if life is hard.
Trust He who made the sun
To chase the clouds of doubt away
And show His will was done.

Margaret Peterson

44

A New Beginning

Now is the time for a new beginning,
Ridding ourselves of all doubts and fears.
Time to move on with faith and forgiving,
Putting aside all grievances and tears.

God is our refuge. His spirit will lead us.
Stress and anxiety no longer here.
All pain is gone; burdens have left us,
Sweet peace is ours. God makes it so clear.

We seek new paths... so joyful and daring.
Talents and gifts we surely will find.
And we'll help others with our compassion.
Negative thoughts are all left behind.

Now is the time for a new beginning –
Knowing through faith all things we can do.
God is our refuge, our Lord, our redeemer.
Jesus, our Savior, makes everything new!

Edna Massimilla

In the beginning was the Word,
and the Word was with God,
and the Word was God.
John 1:1

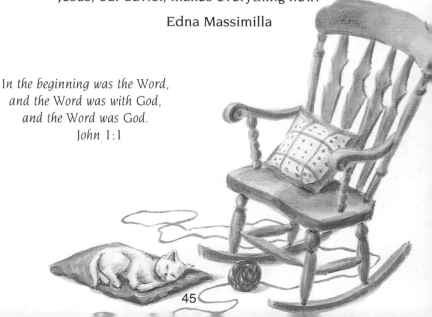

A Winner

Brilliant as sunshine,
The heart that has found
The glory of Heaven,
Seeing God all around.

The darkness has vanished,
The light has come through,
For God in His goodness
Has rewarded you.

Your faith was the jewel
That let the light in,
So now you're a winner
And God let you win.

Continue to practice,
There's much more in store.
Keep shining your faith
For a new open door.

The sky is the limit,
So aim for the gold.
See in each golden moment
A new story unfold.

In awe, you'll be speechless
As the pathway you trod,
And as your faith keeps growing,
You will see more of God.

Chris Zambernard

Another Door Opens

To those who will listen
Through shadows of time,
His words speak of goodness,
Of love, so sublime.
Through trials on earth that
Include pain and tears,
The Lord give us courage…
Erases all fears.
And if one door closes,
We may feel distress,
But the next open door
May bring true happiness.
Let us walk by His side,
Surrounded by light,
Though today may be weary…
Tomorrow will be bright.

Angie Monnens

48

God's
Gift of Spring

Bright sunshine and the beauty of the flowers,
The perfumed breeze that permeates the air,
The meadow polka-dotted now with daisies,
The green-clad hills and soft blue skies so fair…
The leafy trees that line the country roadways,
The merry sound of streams and brooks that flow,
Birds singing sweetly through the golden hours,
The splendor of the sunset's crimson glow…
The host of daffodils that grace the hillsides,
The joy and hope when all the earth is new,
The blossoming trees adorned in pink-white glory,
A rainbow world that gladdens hearts anew…
Yes, Spring has come with all its cherished wonders;
There's so much beauty everywhere we go –
God sends His gift of Spring to please His children,
And show us that He cares and loves us so.

Beverly J. Anderson

Thanks be to God for
His indescribable gift!
2 Corinthians 9:15

Springtime Perfection

I discovered a little white chapel today
As I strolled in the fresh country air.
An old picket fence stood beside it
And flowers were dancing everywhere.

Oh, such a tranquil little meadow
With pink and blue blooms beckoning me near.
They were proudly raising their dainty heads
To proclaim to man, "Springtime is here!"

I walked toward the chapel door –
It seemed such an inspiring place to pray.
I was drawn inside by the silence,
Then the wind made the chapel bells sway.

When I heard the bells begin to chime,
I felt I had entered a special place.
Down on my knees, I went in prayer –
For a while I was lost in time and space.

As I began my walk back down the lane,
I turned to treasure this springtime perfection.
How befitting that I should feel a rebirth –
It's the season of Christ's resurrection!

Barbara Cagle Ray

I have seen the limits of all perfection,
but Your command is without bounds.
Psalm 119:96

I Thank Thee...

I thank Thee, Master, Lord and King,
For dwelling by my side;
When pain and sadness fill my soul,
I feel Thy love abide...

I thank Thee, Master, Lord and King;
My life I give to Thee,
For Thou art always close to me
To set my spirit free...

I thank Thee, Master, Lord and King,
Redeemer of my soul;
I hold Thee ever in my heart;
Come help me reach my goal!

Hope C. Oberhelman

It's Springtime in My Heart

It's springtime in this heart of mine
Regardless of the day or time,
For April sun comes shining through
From out the skies of magic blue.
There are tulips, too, and daffodils
Along the lane where sunshine spills.
It's springtime midst the Summer sun
On country roads where small feet run;
When Autumn changes leaves to gold
Or Winter brings the snow and cold.
Somehow it matters not at all,
For in my heart I hear Spring's call.
The seasons come, the seasons go –
Warm breezes melt the Winter snow.
Atop the hills, a warmth supreme,
So fondly hold each sought-for dream.
I know the Winter will depart…
I've tucked the springtime in my heart.

Garnett Ann Schultz

Everyday Blessings

I once thought that God was only found
In majestic sights and books renowned,
In awesome miracles and symphonies,
In powerful prayers on bended knees.
I found Him in quite everyday things –
The sonorous tones a church bell rings,
The varied trills of a mockingbird,
Young parents' thrill at a child's first word.
He's in fragile snowflakes, fluttering leaves,
Spring's sudden lively raindrops on the eaves,
A compliment given, a problem shared,
The sweet, tender face of one who cared,
In the warm handclasp of a dear, old friend,
And the firm belief that love has no end.

Louise Pugh Corder

A New Beginning

When you pray for a new beginning
And rays of hope appear,
You have a blissful knowledge
That there's a saintly presence near.
In answer to my plea for help,
He sent guidance from above
And now I can see clearly
By His shining light of love.
If I should try again and falter,
I'll know exactly what to do
Because I know He's always with me
Just waiting to see me through.
I know He walks beside me,
I can feel His hand in mine,
And I am forever thankful
To have His love divine.

Orvan Childers

For this is the message you
have heard from the beginning:
we should love one another.
1 John 3:11

Morning Prayer

This day belongs to You, O Lord;
This world is not my own.
So, take my hand and hold it tight
And safely see me home.

The deeds that I perform today
I offer up to You,
To praise and honor Your dear name
In thanks for all You do.

For 'tis to You I owe my life,
The very air I breathe;
The food I eat, the clothes I wear;
My sorrows You relieve.

Without You, Lord, what would I do?
My steps would go astray.
Your love is what I hunger for,
Your light to show the way.

O heavenly Father, hear my plea;
Your mercy on me bestow.
Let love for Jesus fill my heart,
And love to others show.

Leo A. Morgan

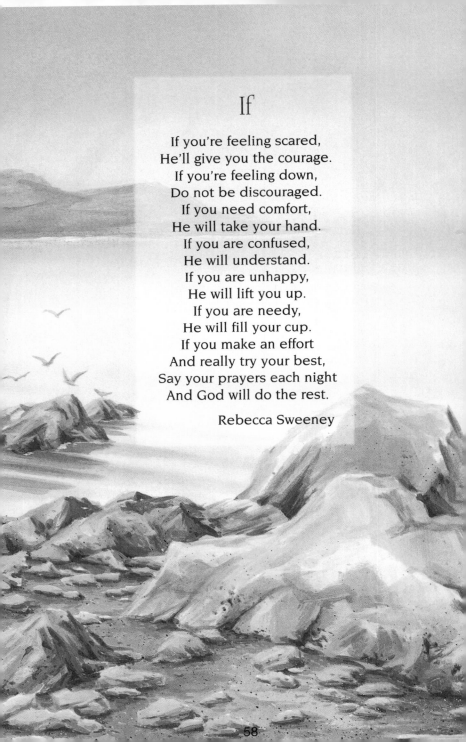

If

If you're feeling scared,
He'll give you the courage.
If you're feeling down,
Do not be discouraged.
If you need comfort,
He will take your hand.
If you are confused,
He will understand.
If you are unhappy,
He will lift you up.
If you are needy,
He will fill your cup.
If you make an effort
And really try your best,
Say your prayers each night
And God will do the rest.

Rebecca Sweeney

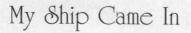

My Ship Came In

When my prayers seem unanswered
And there is a long delay,
I'll cling to the wharves of hope
And keep looking every day…
For the ship laden with treasures
On faith's horizon to appear.
God can hear the faintest whisper
And knows I'm waiting here.
Once the ship has been sighted
And faith's cargo brought ashore,
Weeping I'll thank the Savior
For my answer came once more.

Dottlee Duggan Reid

Smile and Be Happy

Sometimes we get depressed,
Tired of the same routine:
Waking up, getting dressed,
Worry about the unforeseen.

But we all have a duty
To fulfill in our time;
No use for getting angry
For no reason or rhyme.

If we take the bitter
And exchange it for the sweet,
That in itself
Will be the greatest feat.

So smile and be happy
On each God-given day,
And thank Him for His blessings
And whistle on your way.

Josephine March

The Lord has done great
things for us; Oh, how
happy we are!
Psalm 126:3

Look, Listen and Love

Many poems have been written
With words of wisdom and grace;
Some are like chilly north winds,
Others put a smile on your face.
Many pictures have been painted
With colors vivid and bold,
While others offer delicate reflections,
Requiring our silence to behold.
Tones of the universe have been sounded
By harps, trumpets, and bells,
By choruses of men, women and children –
They each have a message to tell.
There are words that have never been spoken,
New songs from the heavens above
And never-seen colors in the rainbow,
If we look, listen and love.

Grace Lee Frank Smith

*Then they believed His words
and sang songs of praise.*
Psalm 106:12

The Answer Is Jesus

The answer is Jesus
To the questions of life.
He's the only solution
To sorrows and strife.

The answer is Jesus
When we lose our way.
He's the anchor we cling to
When we go astray.

The answer is Jesus
To each sinner's prayer.
He died on the cross,
Our burdens to bear.

The answer is Jesus
Each day of the year.
He's the blessed assurance,
We have nothing to fear.

The answer is Jesus
To the questions of life.
He's the only solution
To sorrows and strife.

Clay Harrison

*Answer me, Lord, in Your
generous love; in Your great
mercy turn to me.*
Psalm 69:17

The Little Things

Thank You, Lord, for little things
Like rays of hope a smile can bring,
A clasping of a helping hand,
The soothing words – "I understand,"
The warmth of sunshine after rain,
A sign of comfort after pain!
A friend who stays through trials and tears,
The peace they give to calm our fears,
For all His mercy and His love
When prayers are answered from above.
Oh thank You, Lord, for little things
That help us soar on eagles' wings!

Kathryn Wiesenhoefer

Walk With Me

Oh, walk with me, dear Jesus.
Stay by my side each day.
Help me to carry my burdens
And listen when I pray.

Take my hand and guide me.
Show me the way I should go.
I may not choose the right paths,
But I'm trusting that You will know.

Oh, walk with me, dear Jesus.
Infold me with Your love.
Bestow on me the blessing
That comes from Heaven above.

Keep me ever safe from danger
As I travel along life's way.
I will be forever grateful
Until my dying day.

Mary Ellen Porter Dole

Your love is before my
eyes; I walk guided by
Your faithfulness.
Psalm 26:3

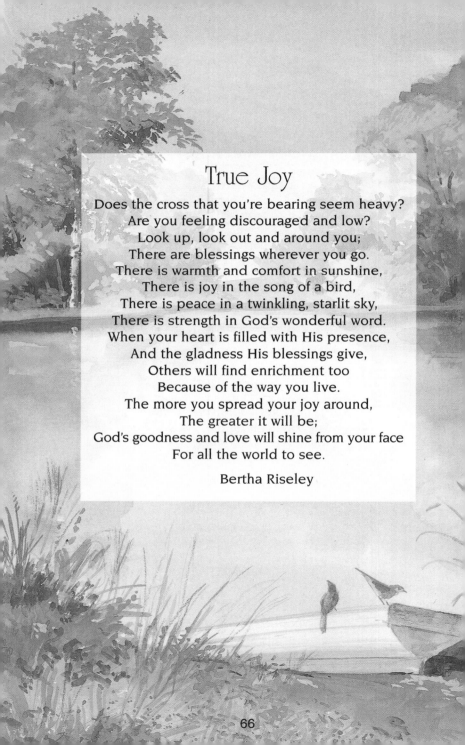

True Joy

Does the cross that you're bearing seem heavy?
Are you feeling discouraged and low?
Look up, look out and around you;
There are blessings wherever you go.
There is warmth and comfort in sunshine,
There is joy in the song of a bird,
There is peace in a twinkling, starlit sky,
There is strength in God's wonderful word.
When your heart is filled with His presence,
And the gladness His blessings give,
Others will find enrichment too
Because of the way you live.
The more you spread your joy around,
The greater it will be;
God's goodness and love will shine from your face
For all the world to see.

Bertha Riseley

Seasons of the Heart

Don't think it strange, this trial you bear,
This mood of darker hue –
For the joys you knew just yesterday
Will soon return to you.

Nature has her changing seasons,
So too the heart of man;
The key to getting through it, though,
Lies right there in your hand...

Stretch forth that hand to someone else;
Yes, pass the key to them;
For in helping someone else you'll find
That's where your joy will stem.

And that one you've helped to find the sun
Now holds the precious key,
And someone else in prison darkness...
Is soon to be set free!

Denise A. DeWald

To every thing there is a season,
and a time to every purpose
under the Heaven.
Ecclesiastes 3:1

My strength and my courage is the
Lord, and He has been my Savior.
He is my God, I praise Him; the
God of my father, I extol Him.
Exodus 15:2

Bridges

When life seems hopeless and dreary,
Don't walk around in sheer despair.
You don't have to cross a bridge alone;
God's presence is always with you there.
Press on with courage toward your goal;
Be steadfast when you must suffer loss.
Trust God and try not to look ahead –
Most bridges you'll never have to cross.

Barbara Cagle Ray

Autumn's Wardrobe

Autumn is wearing a multi-hued dress,
A frock of all colors, her seasonal best.
Each color becomes her, whatever it is...
Red, orange, russet, gold... just part of the list.

Her dress is the forest and countryside fields,
The fields garbed in bountiful harvest yields.
Her autumnal bonnet's the sky overhead,
Enhanced with an autumntide floral sunset.

Her footwear consists of the silvery frost
That's scattered about on the grasses and moss.
Autumn is wearing a color-splashed dress,
Wardrobe of beauty at God's Autumn fest.

Loise Pinkerton Fritz

*Thou crownest the year
with Thy goodness...*
Psalm 65:11

70

Open Your Life

Open your life to see the world
You live in every day;
Hear the songs that fill the air
When people work and play.
Feel the love that blooms and grows
In every form of life;
See the faith that adds to love
In struggle and in strife.

Open your life to see the world
And let the world come in –
See the rays of hope and prayer
That darkness cannot dim.
Open your life to what is yours
To see and hear and know
And find the love God means for you
To harvest, reap and sow.

Michael Dubina

*Open my eyes to see clearly the
wonders of Your teachings.*
Psalm 119:18

Walk With Hope

Eternal life – of this I dream.
Resounding melody – quiet stream.
The seeds of hope bring sunshine near,
Loud songs of joy, my God is here.

He joins the angels one by one,
Forever encased – eternal sun.
Heaven's delight – the joyous rope
Shines brightly on these seeds of hope.

When I was young, I knew no fear,
My God was one, my youthful year.
As I grew older, learned to love,
Cast out the doubt, lived life above.

With angels dancing on my arm,
I knew near God there was no harm,
So I learned to walk and talk and cheer
With Him, my Master very near.

He guides my every step in love.
Holy Spirit – like a dove –
Lifts up my heart like wings of fire…
I walk in love – God, my desire.

Carolyn Fantz

*They that hope in the Lord will renew
their strength, they will soar as with
eagles' wings; they will run and not
grow weary, walk and not grow faint.*
Isaiah 40:31

Thanksgiving

I'm thankful for Nature's seasons
That faithfully come and go,
And for the old and new friends
Good fortune's let me know.
I'm thankful for each helping hand
Or push in the right direction;
And Lord, when I need it most –
Safety in Your protection.
A cozy hearth at eventide
That's shared with those I love
Can always make me conscious
Of Your blessings from above.
But on this day, especially,
I give thanks for everything
That can make a heart happy
And sweet contentment bring.

Catherine Janssen Irwin

A Dream of Winter

I've dreamt of Winters long ago
When on the trees the fallen snow
Appeared as puffs of cotton white
And rabbits burrowed out of sight.
And redbirds in their jaunty red
Flew hither-tither o'er my head
Then sought prized morsels in the snow –
A childhood Winter long ago.
And sleigh bells rang down country lanes,
Crisp snowflakes etched my windowpanes,
Secure at home with fires aglow –
A childhood Winter long ago.
October's gold, November's rain
Now offer promise once again
To bring the season I love so:
December with its welcome snow.
And I stay home by hearth and know
The secret tinge, that heartfelt glow;
My windows frame this world of white
In childhood's dream on Winter's night.

Henry W. Gurley

*Let my prayer come before
You; rescue me according
to Your promise.*
Psalm 119:170

75

Blessings

Please help us, Lord, to trust Your will
When we seek things in prayer.
You know the paths we cannot see –
You'll lead with loving care.

You may not bless us with a crown,
But rather with a cross;
Perhaps with pain, but if Your choice,
We'll count it gain, not loss.

Not always in the way we'd choose,
You bless, yet from Your hand
Can only come the very best
That holds a purpose grand.

So help us, Lord, to ask Your will
When we pray "Bless me, Lord."
Not temporal, but lasting gifts
Will be our rich reward.

Beverly J. Anderson

A Kingdom of My Own

Upon a sparkling, wintry morn
As snow in graceful flight
Designs its flakes in lacy weave
And all my world turns white…
I rise to greet the wonders of
This season now full-blown,
And find a realm of fantasy,
A kingdom of my own.

My cottage all aglitter, and
My forests twice aglow;
My lamp shines golden in my room;
I seek no place to go.
Upon a sparkling wintry morn
My thoughts, my dreams conspire;
Outside the snowflakes lacy white –
Inside a warming fire!

Henry W. Gurley

*Jesus, however, called the children to
Himself and said, "Let the children come
to Me and do not prevent them; for the
Kingdom of God belongs to such as these."
Luke 18:16*

God Is

If there is a God in Heaven,
Does He hear us when we call?
Does He heed our supplication?
Does He care for us at all?

Yes, there is a God in Heaven,
Though it's not some far-off place.
He is waiting close beside us
With His love and boundless grace.

You may think that you're forgotten,
That your name He can't recall
Or He's gone away and left you
Or He wasn't there at all.

His answer may elude you;
Human eyes can't always see.
Something better may be coming
And the best is yet to be.

Keep on calling, keep on trusting,
For a loving God is there.
Your faith is what is missing
When He does not answer prayer.

Mabel Warburton

*Grace to you and peace from
God our Father and the
Lord Jesus Christ.*
1 Corinthians 1:3

Souvenirs

I have a collection of springtime things:
A blue sky filled with feathered wings,
Thistledown upon the breeze,
And the fragile pink of cherry trees.
I have a collection of Summer things:
A brown stone wall where the ivy clings,
A forest pool in a grassy glen
With cool green shadows peeping in.
I have a collection of Autumn things:
Frosty mornings, grey smoke rings,
Silver rain on rustic eaves
And winding lanes of golden leaves.
I have a collection of Winter things:
A cozy fire and a pot that sings,
Moonlight on new fallen snow,
The sunset's coral afterglow.
Such are my treasures packed with care
In my memory trunk of yesteryear.
How glad I am that I thought to take
Them with me, lest my heart should break,
And my back grow tired, and my footsteps slow,
And my hands reach out for the long ago.
And they are why I can recall
And know that life was worth it all!

Grace E. Easley

A Lifetime of Miracles

Each day brings forth new miracles
Of sun and sea and sky.
Another bird bursts from his shell
And spreads his wings to fly.

New growth, new life is everywhere.
Each bright day will unfold
Fresh opportunities for all...
And worth their weight in gold.

The Master gazes down on us
As He brings forth the dawn
And blesses each and every one
With courage to go on.

Marian Ford Park

God indeed is my Savior; I am
confident and unafraid. My
strength and my courage is the
Lord, and He has been my Savior.
Isaiah 12:2

Anywhere, Everywhere

Teach me to so worship, Lord,
That I concentrate on Thee,
Forgetting these surroundings,
Using eyes of faith to see.

In a resplendent cathedral
Resounding hymns of praise;
With stained glass light illumined,
My whispered thanks I raise.

Or by a tranquil lakeside
With azure sky a dome.
You inhabit all the earth
So I can feel at home.

With throngs of believers
Or in stark solitude,
You speak in Your word
And feed me holy food.

So I draw near to worship
And leave all else behind;
Come, blessed Holy Spirit,
And fill my yielded mind.

         Elaine Hardt

Make known to me Your ways,
Lord; teach me Your paths.
Psalm 25:4

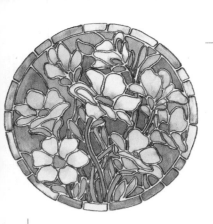

Welcome in Spring

This morning is lovely,
The sun is so bright,
The daffodils surely
Are such a grand sight.

The birds in the treetop
Are singing their song;
In welcome to springtime,
Let's all sing along.

The grass on the lawn
Needs a clipping or two;
It seems to be heavy
With diamond-like dew.

Oh welcome in springtime,
Come show off your face;
It's glowing with beauty
And sweet, loving grace.

Katherine Smith Matheney

God's
Glorious Springtime

The Winter is past and the rain is gone,
A sunrise explodes in brilliant dawn.
God's flowers appear all over the earth,
The singing of birds reveal their sweet worth.

The voice of the dove is heard in our land –
Message of springtime is soothing and grand!
Concerts of robins as they build their homes,
Bees buzzing loudly to shape honeycombs.

God touches blossoms with new pastel brush,
Each fragrant petal creates tender hush!
So velvet each blade of grass in the sod –
Truly a miracle born of our God!

Snowdrops and crocus shoot up through the ground,
And shiny, new leaves all rustle around –
Raindrops and sunshine paint rainbows so bright,
God hath made springtime a glorious sight!

Hazel M. Blough

Shout joyfully to God, all you on
earth; sing of His glorious name;
give Him glorious praise.
Psalm 66:1-2

For Eyes to See

The sparkle of a diamond
In the early morning dew,
The softest colors in the sky
When dawn is breaking through...

The shape of a thousand snowflakes
As they fall from the sky,
The pattern God created
To dress a butterfly...

The web a spider weaves
As delicate as lace,
The beauty of wild flowers
In their strangest resting place...

The colors of a rainbow,
The fleecy clouds above –
He makes this for us to see;
He makes it with such love.

A humble heart is filled with joy
For His beauty everywhere,
And takes time out from busy hours
To kneel to Him in prayer.

Edna Fontaine

Holy men of humble heart,
bless the Lord; praise and
exalt Him above all forever.
Daniel 3:87

The Season Called Spring

Soft shades of green
Cover hedges and trees.
Newly-born lambs
Walk on wobbling knees.
The brown sod is tilled
To receive precious seed.
Bread for the sower,
To meet every need.
Children at play
In the sun's warm light,
Dirt on their faces,
Eyes shining bright.
Rainbows and puddles,
Birds on the wing…
Hope is unending
In the season called Spring.

Regina Wiencek

Abundant Life

Speak kindly every time you speak,
Search wisely for the dreams you seek,
Be gentle with the ones you love,
And always look to God above,
Still keep faith from day to day,
And ever walk a goodly way.

Life is brief, so live it well.
Within your heart, sweet dreams will dwell;
Always share a friendly smile,
Happiness makes life worthwhile,
Be helpful to a soul in need,
'Tis good to do a kindly deed.

New beginnings, bright new dawn,
Drewdrops sparkle on the lawn.
Prayer, believing – both a must
To a God we ever trust.
Happy moments – free of strife –
Giving us abundant life.

Garnett Ann Schultz

*Moreover, God is able to make
every grace abundant to you, so
that in all things, always having
all you need, you may have an
abundance for every good work.*
2 Corinthians 9:8

I See
God Everywhere

I see God in the morning
When the sun begins to rise
And in a touch of Heaven
In a newborn baby's eyes.

I see God in each tiny flower
That blooms along my way
And in the little children near,
So happy at their play.

I see God in each friendly smile
That cheers a lonely heart
And in each act of kindness
With warm blessings to impart.

In colored leaves and snowflakes,
Each pretty songbird near,
I see God in the farm scene,
Wee cuddly lambs so dear.

I see God in a Summer sky
Of softest azure hue;
In the red-gold flame of sunset,
His face comes shining through.

No matter where I chance to look
When skies are dark or fair,
My God is never far away...
I see Him everywhere.

Kay Hoffman

Bless the Lord, all creatures,
everywhere in God's domain.
Bless the Lord, my soul!
Psalm 103:22

A Sunflower Prayer

I prayed as I looked toward the eastern sky,
"Lord, make me useful as the day goes by,"
And then, at high noon, I looked up above
And asked Him to give me a heart full of love.

At sunset, I asked for a place in the sun;
My happy heart sang, He had given me one!
Then I walked with Him down a sunflowered lane
Saying, "Thank You, dear God, again and again."

Laura Baker Haynes

We Thank Thee, Lord...

We thank Thee, Lord, for this new day
And all the joy it brings;
We thank Thee for Thy precious gifts
And for each bird that sings...

We thank Thee, Lord, for this new day
And for Thy love and hope;
We thank Thee for Thy precious care
And for the strength to cope...

We thank Thee, Lord, for this new day;
Come fill our hearts with peace.
We need Thee, oh our gracious King;
Please grant us Thy release...

We thank Thee, Lord, for this new day;
Grant us Thy special care.
Hold us, dear Master, in Thy hand,
And listen to our prayer.

Hope C. Oberhelman

*If you and your children are well
and your affairs are going as well as
you wish, I thank God very much,
for my hopes are in Heaven.*
2 Maccabees 9:20

The Window of Tomorrow

The window of tomorrow
God keeps covered from our view,
But no matter what may be,
His light comes shining through.

God knows our human frailty
And because He loves us so
Gives us light for each new day,
The future not to know.

So, worry not about the morrow,
Live in God's light this day.
Its precious moments come not again,
Don't let them slip away.

Be not anxious about tomorrow,
For soon it will become today
Bringing with it God's guiding light
To direct the uncertain way.

One day the window will become a door,
A portal that opens the way
To God's eternal holy light
Where our light with His will stay!

Josephine Anne Miller

It's Up to Me

I have a choice this morning
As I get out of bed
To put a smile upon my face,
Or choose to frown instead.

To bring a bit of laughter,
A little bit of cheer,
To hurting, hungry, weary souls,
To show them God is near.

All of us have problems
As we go about our day.
May we always think of others
To help them on life's way.

Mary Ann Jameson

*You are near, O Lord; reliable
are all Your commands.*
Psalm 119:151

I Thank Thee

I thank Thee for the morning sun,
For twilight hours when day is done,
For afternoons all warm and bright,
The stars within the still of night,
For April rain and birds that sing,
The beauties of the shining Spring.

I thank Thee for the blue of sky,
For valleys low and mountains high,
The Autumn colors – red and gold,
For Summer sun and Winter cold,
A country lane where wildflowers grow,
A crocus blooming in the snow.

For dreams to dream and laughter sweet
And every friend I chance to meet,
The many blessings that are mine,
A hope complete – a faith divine,
For all the love You give to me…
Dear God above, my thanks to Thee.

Garnett Ann Schultz

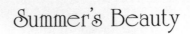

Summer's Beauty

Where the golden hills of daisies
Meet the trickling stream nearby,
The wild flowers sway under stately trees
That reach toward the sapphire sky.

The earth's fresh, green carpet
That stretches across the land,
Adds beauty to the Summer
And was made by God's loving hand.

The gentle breeze that scatters the seeds
Across the fresh plowed earth,
Soon will spring through broken sod
And burst forth with new birth.

The beautiful robin's red breast
Brings joy into my heart.
The songbirds sing their serenade
While fledglings from nest depart.

The fragrant flowers are abundant.
They bring pleasure and delight.
I'll always be thankful for Summer
For making life sunny and bright.

Shirley Hile Powell

I will delight and rejoice in
You; I will sing hymns to
Your name, Most High.
Psalm 9:3

The Gentle Folk

Some folk have a gentle way
With warm words to impart;
They seem to know just what to say
To ease an aching heart.

They never are too busy
To take a little time
To share another's load of care
When hills are hard to climb.

And when your heart is happy
Their hearts are happy, too,
Because they've helped make someone's sky
A little bit more blue.

Thank You, God, for gentle folk
We meet from day to day;
Our world's a sweeter, brighter place
Because they passed our way.

Kay Hoffman

My Hope

My hope lies not in wealth or fame,
But in the power of Jesus' name.

In His name, I can do all things;
I'm lifted up on eagle's wings.

My faith is placed in things above;
My heart is filled with His love.

He gives me strength when I am weak;
His spirit fills me when I speak.

He told me, "Go and sin no more!"
I'm not the man I was before.

He gives me drink and daily bread,
For by His grace, we all are fed.

When I am still, I hear His voice;
My Master's will shall be my choice.

My hope lies not in wealth or fame,
But in the power of Jesus' name!

Clay Harrison

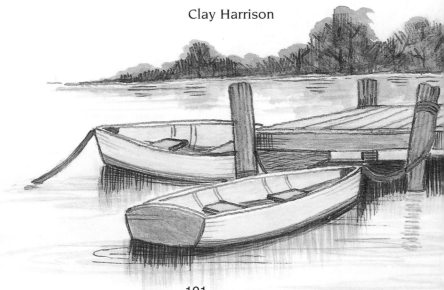

A Summer Day

The morning stood all bathed in dew
Beneath the vast expanse of blue.
The day, exquisite to behold,
Brought new visions to my soul.
The air was warm and motionless;
The world seemed void of all distress.
Unbroken thoughts, a prayer or two –
'Tis God's reflection shining through.

Gene Appleby

The Splendor of Your Glory

Lord, I see the splendor of Your glory
As I gaze across the land.
I know it is a glimpse of You,
For it was made by Your own hand.

I see Your love in every flower
And in the majestic mountains high.
I see it in the seasons that change
And in every bird that flies.

I see it in the babbling brook
And in the grassy fields of green.
I see it in the canyons deep
And in the tranquil country scenes.

Your love for us must be so great
That nothing else would do
But to give to us Your very best
To enjoy our whole lives through.

Shirley Hile Powell

*Give to the Lord the glory due
God's name. Bow down before
the Lord's holy splendor!*
Psalm 29:2

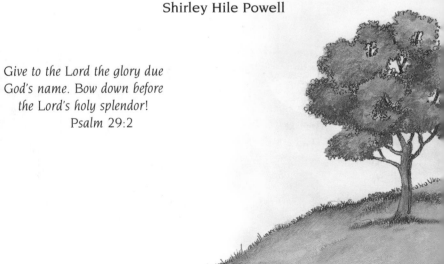

Prayers of a Faithful Friend

Sometimes life seems o'erwhelming,
Troubles weigh heavy on my mind;
Peace then seems as elusive
As a treasure, hard to find.

The faith that once sustain'd me
Is like a distant memory,
And I question if God in Heaven
Has somehow forgotten me.

Then I feel His gentle presence
As the brush of angel's wings;
His tender reassurance
To my heart a warmness brings.

Drying all my tears,
He stays 'til doubt has been displaced;
Every fear is banished
And every doubt erased.

Speaking quietly to my spirit,
He breathes newness into me;
Restoring by His mercy
My threatened security.

And I hear His still, small voice,
"My child, soon this trial shall end";
Somehow I know He is responding
To prayers of a faithful friend.

Mary Mizrany

"Do not let your hearts be troubled.
You have faith in God…"
John 14:1

Autumn's on Her Way

Today I left ajar my white terrace door
And a breeze came sweeping down the hall.
Along with the wind, fluttering leaves of gold –
God's telegram to announce the coming Fall.
I felt a small, fleeting twinge of grief
To see golden leaves among the bright green,
And the petals of the last rose of Summer
Were flying 'round outside the window screen.
Like all the seasons, Autumn's Heaven-sent;
Summer moves out and she parades in.
As God's hand keeps turning the axis of time,
She'll revolve around and greet us again.
Leaves of green will flame the lighted torches,
And Autumn will create a dazzling display.
Mums are now glowing in colorful beds;
Goodbye, Summer – Autumn's on her way!

Barbara Cagle Ray

Autumn Walks With God

Dearest Autumn arrives in a rush
With color to paint the trees –
Her garment is woven with threads of change,
Her pockets billow with the breeze.

Her sandals trace idyllic days
O'er skies the bluest to see –
She blows cool respite on the land,
Whereas Summer ran merry and free.

Dearest Autumn brings a huge moon
To shine on the harvest crop –
Fresh, crisp air and hoarfrost nights
Make the temperature drop.

She carries a basket of bounty
Culled from the depth of the soil –
And hand in hand, she walks with God,
Rewarding mankind for its toil.

Gael Phaneuf

*For at the proper time we
will reap a harvest.*
Galatians 6:9

A Touch of Autumn

A touch of red, a touch of gold,
A tapestry of Autumn bold.
A patchwork quilt of falling fire
October wears for her attire.
A touch of green, a touch of blue,
A sapphire sky of brilliant hue.
A multitude of mums parade
Across Fall's scenic cavalcade.
A touch of frost, a touch of sun,
A changing season just begun.
A crispy, crimson-colored morn –
These Autumn gifts are Heaven-born.

Nora M. Bozeman

In Return

You asked, "What can I do for you?"
The gesture meant so much,
For in my hour of greatest need,
You came to lift me up.

My broken heart was evident
In tears that would not end,
But you were there to give me hope,
And be my faithful friend.

Other folks had tried as well
To reach out to me back then,
But only you could get inside
And comfort this old friend.

If winds of grief begin to blow,
As in life they often do,
I'll be asking you the same...
"What can I do for you?"

Jill Lemming

When cares increase within me,
Your comfort gives me joy.
Psalm 94:19

A Vista of Autumn

Sheer beauty veils the countryside
Since autumntide is here.
The dew is sparkling everywhere,
The morns are crisp and clear.

In stretching fields, the amber grain
Waves gently to and fro.
The trailing vines bear pumpkins orange;
On cornstalks, ears hang low.

The ripened fruit dots orchard trees
On these autumnal days,
And roadside stands are everywhere
With harvest yields displayed.

The harvest moon sheds moonbeams bright
Upon the old feed mill,
While the water wheel turns 'round and 'round
Amidst the Autumn chill.

The husking bees are in full swing
In barns across the land;
It is a time of thanks and joy,
A time of song and dance.

Sheer beauty dons the countryside
As hearts with cheer abound
Upon God's Autumn time of year,
The time with goodness crowned.

Loise Pinkerton Fritz

Thanks to Jesus

More and more – as days grow weary
And we age and live alone –
We can only find life's comforts
In the prayers that we intone.
Friends and loved ones God has taken
To His kingdom in the sky,
And we live with what is left us
Of the loves that hurried by.

Thanks to Jesus – Lord and Savior –
Who gives comfort to our prayers
And endears us in our heartaches
When we cry in life's despairs.
Thanks to Him who feels our sorrows
And our loneliness of heart
To endear us with His blessings
And the comforts faith imparts.

Michael Dubina

*Hallelujah! Give thanks to
the Lord, who is good,
whose love endures forever.*
Psalm 106:1

Promises

God doesn't give the rainbow
Before He sends the showers.
He always sends Winter's cold
Before the springtime flowers.
God has never promised
Our days will all be fair;
He only has promised
That He is always there.

When the rain begins to fall
And the days are not so bright,
When the storm clouds gather
And a chill comes in the night...
Remember God's promises
Are faithful and are true.
No matter what the day may bring
The Lord is there with you.

Ruth J. Tabberer

*The promises of the Lord I will
sing forever, proclaim Your
loyalty through all ages.*
Psalm 89:2

On Kindness

Kind words accomplish miracles,
Where threats fall on deaf ears.
No one is ever ruled through fear...
However it appears.
No matter what the challenge is
Or choices we must make,
Each one of us must choose the path
Our feet are meant to take.

How often we have criticized
What we don't understand,
Claimed God's right to judgement...
Which was not given man.
Imagined that "we know it all"
And in our foolish pride,
Accepted tales as true before...
We know the other side.

Dear Lord, forgive our blindness,
Who see ourselves as strong,
Teach us, though we're often right...
That we are sometimes wrong.
Help us to keep in good repair
This small glass house we own,
And grant our hands be quick to help...
But never throw a stone.

Grace E. Easley

Autumn Sunrise

How beautiful the sunrise
Against the Autumn skies
Where streaks of mauve and charcoal
Dance before my eyes.
How silently the Artist
Paints His masterpiece.
And hangs it in the heavens
Where sunbeams never cease.
Each sunrise is a treasure,
Each cloud is silver-lined…
Each painting hangs forever
On the canvas of my mind.

Clay Harrison

You Took the Time

You took the time to be my friend
Although I was shut in.
You came into my meager world
And left a glow within.

Your flowers brightened up my room
And helped my spirits, too.
You gave the gift of kindliness
When I was feeling blue.

You took the time to sense my need,
To comfort and to share;
How I thank God you stopped my way
And took the time to care.

Beverly J. Anderson

There Is Music

There is music all around us
In the meadow, vast and wide,
In the city streets so busy
And the quiet countryside.
You can hear the notes so lovely
If you listen with your heart,
And the whole wide world is gladdened
In the notes that life imparts.

There is music on the hilltop
'Neath a sky of brightest blue,
In the wonders shared by Nature
And the cotton cloudsteps, too,
In the silent hours of nighttime
Or the breaking hours of dawn,
In the happiness of dewdrops
As they sparkle on the lawn.

God above – the master player –
Fills His world with life and song
In the joyous sound of laughter,
Precious notes, so sweet and strong.
Smiling down on earth's warm beauty,
Part of every star above,
Listening hearts will always hear it…
Music filled with endless love.

Garnett Ann Schultz

*Sing praise, play music; proclaim
all His wondrous deeds!*
Psalm 105:2

He Comes to Us...

He comes to us in the smallest things –
Our Lord, with all His mighty power.
He's the wind beneath the wings of a bird,
And the fragrance of just one tiny flower.

He comes to hover over the ocean's waves,
In the beauty of a radiant Summer night.
He stands amidst the fields of golden grain
As the sun pours down its endless light.

He comes in the furred and gentle creatures
Who stare at the world through innocent eyes.
Can you not feel His presence in the breeze
Or see His twinkle in the starlit skies?

He comes shining through misty Summer skies
When the rainbow smiles and brightly glows.
He's the vine that climbs the flower trellis
With buds, like folded hands, that yield a rose.

He comes to us on snow-filled Winter days
As flakes fly from above on silent wings.
God surrounds us each and every day –
He comes to us in the smallest things!

Barbara Cagle Ray

For You

I thought of you today
And said a little prayer;
I felt an answer in my heart
And knew that He was there.

I did not ask for wealth or fame
And I knew you wouldn't mind;
I asked Him to send treasures
Of a far more lasting kind.

I asked that He be near you
At the start of each new day
To grant you health and blessings
And friends to share your way.

I asked for happiness for you
In all things, great and small,
But it was for His loving care
That I prayed for most of all.

Glenn Jacobs

No treasure greater than a
healthy body; no happiness,
than a joyful heart!
Sirach 30:16

My Silent Partner

God is always with me,
No matter where I go.
He is my silent partner
And I love Him so.

He walks with me in quiet solitude
Across the years of time
And gives me strength and courage
And a peaceful state of mind.

His breath is in the wind
Blowing through the meadows of gold.
His warmth is in the sunlight
That touches the earth below.

His tears are in the raindrops
That come from the sky above,
As He gently showers the earth
With His blessings and His love.

Yes, God is my silent partner,
My Savior and my friend,
And He is always with me
From dawn's first light to night's end.

Mary Grace Patterson

Sounds of Winter

The Winter sounds are many;
Too, they're diversified.
They echo through the morning,
The noontide and the night.

There's neighing of the horses,
Pulling horse-drawn sleighs
Across the open meadows
And down the country lanes.

Then there's the wind a-howling
As Winter storms arrive,
Bringing heap-high snowfalls
Which are each child's delight.

Too, there's the shout of skaters
Down at the old mill pond.
Through Summer months they waited
To know this Winter fun.

There's laughter of the children
A-sleighing on the hills
And building top-hat snowmen
With all the fancy frills.

We hear the sounds of Winter
Amidst the wintry chill;
Basking in each one of them –
That makes God's days joy-filled.

Loise Pinkerton Fritz

Out of the south cometh the whirlwind:
and cold out of the north.
Job 37:9

I Am My Brother's Keeper

My heart aches for those who hurt
And cannot find release,
For those who mourn throughout the night
And cannot sleep in peace.

I sympathize with those who fear
The coming of each day,
Those who somehow lost their way
And hurt too much to pray.

I cry for those whose tears are dry
As they reach out to me,
And pray that through the eyes of faith
I'm strong enough to see.

For I am my brother's keeper,
Whoever he may be,
And I pray that when I'm hurting
My brother comforts me.

Clay Harrison

"Am I my brother's keeper?"
Genesis 4:9

Cardinals in the Snow

My birdfeeder is freshly filled with food;
I can see animal tracks in the crusted snow.
Icicles are hanging from the boughs of the trees;
Droplets of water trickle to the earth below.

Such a frosty fantasy is a delight to behold;
Feathers are flying outside my windowpane.
Like sentinels, birds line the tops of the roofs.
Which one will be first to sample the grain?

There soon alights a royal-crested cardinal
To delight in the new-found Winter treat.
He cocks his frosted head of scarlet red
And flits furiously around on his tiny feet.

He eats his fill, then sails to the ground;
Red feathers flutter in the white luster below.
The north wind whispers in the distant pines –
I love Winter and cardinals in the snow!

Barbara Cagle Ray

And as he sowed, some seed
fell on the path, and the
birds came and ate it up.
Mark 4:4

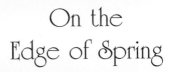

On the
Edge of Spring

I thought I heard a robin sing;
It seemed it could not be,
But then I spied him proudly perched
On bough of leafless tree.

The sky was drear and overcast,
The lacy snowflakes fell.
Upon my winter-weary heart,
He cast his magic spell.

He didn't need the sun to shine,
His happy song did ring;
I think the angels must have joyed
To hear that wee bird sing.

With humble heart, I listened there
Until he flew away.
He never knew the cheer he brought
To others on that day.

How caring is our loving God
Who sends the bird to sing
When the heart's grown winter-weary
Just on the edge of Spring!

Kay Hoffman

When Winter Comes

Majestic mountains that rise above
The valleys down below,
With snow-capped peaks that spiral high
To catch the Fall's first snow.
Fall's foliage, ablaze with color,
Must recede to second place,
For soon, the snows of Winter
Will come with all their grace.
Earth's carpet will lie pressed beneath it –
This shroud of pristine snow –
To lie there in dormant surrender
'Til Spring comes to bid Winter go.
As the village prepares to greet him,
Old-Man Winter with his blanket of white –
The villagers, once more, have resigned themselves
To many a long wintry night.

Mary S. Chevalier